MEDWAY
SHIPPING
FROM FRIGATES TO
FREIGHTERS

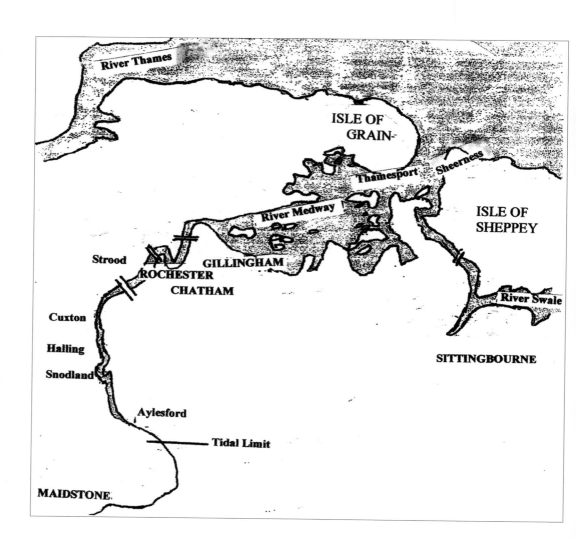

MEDWAY
SHIPPING
FROM FRIGATES TO
FREIGHTERS

GEOFF LUNN

TEMPUS

Frontispiece: The River Medway, from tidal limit to estuary. (Maps in the book are hand drawn by the author).

First published 2005

Tempus Publishing Limited
The Mill, Brimscombe Port,
Stroud, Gloucestershire, GL5 2QG
www.tempus-publishing.com

British Library Cataloguing in Publication Data.
A catalogue record for this book is available from the British Library.

ISBN 0 7524 3565 5

Typesetting and origination by Tempus Publishing Limited.
Printed in Great Britain.

Contents

Acknowledgements

My thanks are extended to the following people and organisations for their help in the compilation of this book; for their provision of photographs for reproduction, for their invaluable advice and information, and for arranging photographic opportunities: the Medway Archives & Local Studies Centre Illustrations Collection; Chatham Historic Dockyard; Medway Ports; the Kent Messenger Group; BP/Castrol Archives; Rochester Bridge Wardens Trust; Foster Yeoman Ltd; John Bradley, former Director of Thomas Watson (Shipping) Ltd; Laurence Dunn; Terry Bolton; Rochester Cameras and Fotoflite; Roy Brooks of Scotline; and Keith Gravestock of Convoys.

Dedicated to the lives of Edward ('Ted') Lunn and Matthew ('Matt') Smith, father and father-in-law, without whose interest and influence I would not have begun this, my second book.

Introduction

The River Medway, Kent's principal waterway, rises in sandstone country just over the border with Sussex and meanders for some seventy miles in a north-easterly direction before flowing into the estuary of the River Thames. Always the bridesmaid to London's more illustrious river, the Medway has nevertheless been regarded for many centuries as a safe and secure haven for shipping.

In Roman times the Medway was known as *Fluminus Meduwaeias*, a name believed to have been derived from the ancient English words *medu,* meaning mead, and *wey,* meaning water, so probably referring to the sweetness of its water. There is evidence that the Romans constructed Rochester's first bridge and whilst the exact date will probably never be known, somewhere approaching two thousand years later Rochester is still the furthest point downstream at which the River Medway is bridged.

Although the Romans played an important part in the Medway's history, stamping their indelible impression on the county of Kent and, indeed, most of Britain, it was King Henry VIII in the sixteenth century who paved the way towards the Medway's long-running connections with the Royal Navy. The first English monarch to order the building of ships specifically designed for war, he appreciated the virtues of the river's lower reaches at Chatham as the perfect shelter for his valued fleet, basing a number of vessels there in the winter months. Soon, an Order dated 1550 stipulated that every Royal ship should be harboured in the Medway.

Three years before this, the recorded history of Chatham Dockyard had begun with the rental of a storehouse 'on Jillingham Water'. Further dock buildings were added and Queen Elizabeth I, anxious to enforce a satisfactory defence for the nation's fleet, ordered the construction of fortifications in the shape of Upnor Castle, which has stood to this day on the banks of the Medway opposite the Dockyard site since finally being completed in 1571.

Upnor Castle failed dismally in its attempt to repel the might of the Dutch fleet in 1667. A year later it became a magazine supplying gunpowder and munitions to men o'war moored in the Medway estuary. Nowadays it is open to the public from spring to autumn.

Hoo Fort, located on Hoo Island, where British block ships were sunk and a chain was extended across the Medway in an unsuccessful attempt to stop the Dutch reaching Chatham.

Elizabeth's opinion that defences should be improved was vindicated in the next important phase in the River Medway's history. Chatham Dockyard had entered into shipbuilding with the launch of a thirty-two-gun frigate, the *Constant Warwick*, by the time war with the Dutch had broken out in 1652. War was still raging in 1665 when Samuel Pepys, as Secretary to the Navy, recommended the construction of a small dockyard at Sheerness for the cleaning and repairing of warships. The dockyard and a protective fort were under development in 1667 when the Dutch fleet, under Admiral de Ruyter, sailed into the Medway, easily destroying the yard and its fort, and sinking sixteen British ships.

At Hoo Island and adjacent mudflats the British scuttled several of their own ships in an attempt to block the Dutch fleet on their passage towards Chatham Dockyard. A chain was stretched across the river as a further barrier, but this was broken by the Dutch, who proceeded to refloat sunken British ships that they then took back to Holland. They even had the impertinence to capture the *Royal Charles,* pride of the British Navy. The Dutch raid was the perfect opportunity for Upnor Castle to prove its worth, but it failed pathetically, for so neglected was its state that only four guns were fit for use against the might of the invading fleet.

At least the disastrous outcome of the Dutch raid brought home to the British Government how radically deficient Chatham Dockyard was in terms of manpower and organisation. Corruption was rife, but improvements over subsequent years were such that the Chatham base developed into the country's premier dockyard. Shipbuilding and ship repair work continued and even Sheerness Dockyard turned to shipbuilding, albeit on a much smaller scale. Ships were made of wood and a developing Medway trade was the carriage of English oak from Kentish Weald forests downriver to the dockyards. Also from the Weald were iron goods such as ships' cannon, cast in furnaces.

As large men o'war emerged from dockyard slipways they rubbed shoulders with sailing barges and small hoys making their way to and from upriver locations such as Tonbridge and Maidstone, passing through the restrictive arches of Rochester's medieval bridge on the way. In 1741 the first full load of coal was transported to Tonbridge by the Medway Navigation Company at a selling price of just five pence per hundredweight. Thanks to Chatham Dockyard's increased importance, Rochester began to import Baltic softwood, a trade which continued well into the nineteenth century, resulting in visits to the Medway by attractive sea-going sailing vessels. Cargoes of timber are handled at Rochester even today, centuries after the very first consignments, but no longer for the purpose of shipbuilding.

The River Medway has not only been regarded as a busy waterway and safe anchorage, but was once of value for fishing, or, to be more precise, oysters beds. For hundreds of years oysters provided the river with the opportunity to supply important London and Dutch markets, the industry controlled by an Admiralty Court from Rochester, granted in 1446 by Henry VI to the Admiral of the Medway, who was the Mayor. Nowadays the Mayor of the Medway towns still continues the tradition of beating the bounds, sailing each summer with the Rochester Cruising Club, accompanied by other small craft, to Garrison Point at Sheerness.

The eighteenth and nineteenth centuries saw a strengthening of links between the dockyards of Chatham and Sheerness and the Royal Navy, and of all the ships built at Chatham over a span of three centuries, the most famous was undoubtedly HMS *Victory*, launched in 1765. Nelson's close ties with the Medway were maintained even after his death at Trafalgar, when his body was brought back by his flagship to Sheerness. The war with France encouraged much naval activity on the Medway and within the dockyards, Chatham constructing ships at a rapid pace. In 1813 Sheerness Dockyard was reconstructed with new foundations and a new outer wall, the basis of today's dock system.

Rochester Bridge c.1820. The medieval bridge had stood since 1392. It had just undergone alterations, including the addition of a balustrade, which was later used in the construction of Rochester Esplanade, when the bridge was replaced in 1856. Sail barges would need to lower their gear in order to 'shoot' the Bridge on the river's current, receiving assistance from hufflers, considered to be nothing more than local rogues, who would join the craft as extra crew.

Part of a flotilla of boats accompanying the Mayor of Medway during the annual Admiral's Cruise from Rochester to Sheerness.

It was around this time that Chatham Dockyard faced competition from other Medway-based shipyards, particularly that of Charles and Mary Ross at Acorn Wharf in Rochester. From 1791 to 1814 their yard was busy with the construction of frigates and larger seventy-four-gun ships for the British Navy, although, ironically their first main build was a French frigate, *Le Amiable*. Several merchant vessels for the Hudson Bay Company were also built at Acorn Wharf, which exists today as Rochester's principal ship repair facility.

As the nineteenth century progressed, sail turned to steam and wood to iron. In 1863 a 9,820-ton screw battleship, the *Achilles*, was launched, the first iron ship to be built at Chatham Dockyard. More vessels of similar size were to follow and it was soon apparent that the Dockyard needed to be drastically enlarged to accommodate this new breed of warship. By 1864, after two years' work, the Dockyard had received its first major extension since 1618, the addition of a 380-acre site to its existing ninety-seven acres. This involved the purchase of St Mary's Island and the completed work comprised the formation of three large dock basins and four adjacent graving docks, together with a new river wall and embankment. Chatham Dockyard had now reached its maximum size, which would be retained for the rest of its working life.

Where British fighting ships were once built: a wide variety of coastal and river vessels are overhauled at Rochester's Acorn Wharf.

This was an influential time for the River Medway, for not only were some of the world's largest warships taking to its waters but there was a notable influx of merchant shipping due to the evolution of three local industries – the manufacture of paper, cement and bricks. All these industries were to rely on water transport for the supply of raw materials, fuel and the distribution of finished products.

Once Mr Samuel Hook and his son Charles Townsend Hook had acquired and developed a paper mill at Snodland, between Rochester and Maidstone, in 1854, paper manufacturing quickly became the leading industry on the banks of the Medway. English china clay, esparto grass from Spain and coal would be conveyed upriver in vast quantities and in 1921 a second large mill was opened by Albert E. Reed further upstream near Aylesford.

The advent of cement and brick factories led to an industrial Medway infested by tall, belching chimneys and grey dust. In 1861 the first Portland Cement works opened near Rochester and one of the world's largest cement factories was completed by the Burham Brick Cement and Lime Company in 1880. By the beginning of the twentieth century no fewer than twenty-six cement works lined the Medway riverbanks between Burham and Rainham, which should be of no surprise as the basic requirements for cement making were already to hand: mud and clay from the river's saltings and chalk from adjacent hillsides.

Many fine buildings still exist from the days of considerable development within Chatham Dockyard in the eighteenth and nineteenth centuries, although some require updating and repair.

Looking upriver from Chatham to Rochester, the frozen Medway during the excessively severe winter of 1895.

Photographed c. 1900, the next Rochester Bridge, designed by Sir William Cubitt and completed in 1856. At the far end on the Strood side was a swing portion with a clear opening of more than 15m, allowing the passage of large vessels. However, following a bad accident to one of the arch supports in 1896, the bridge was heightened by nearly 2m. The rebuilt structure was opened in 1914 and remains the present bridge for road traffic travelling in the direction of London.

Most factories would have four or five barges working from the clay beds and the biggest cement and brick manufacturers frequently had their own fleets of spritsail barges for the movement of their finished products. Consequently, amidst the smoke and grime of a working river, there was a healthy demand for new barges, most of which were built in the Rochester area, which became the centre of the barge trade.

By now, a cast iron Rochester Bridge had replaced the stone medieval bridge, which had stood over the Medway for 464 years, allowing more elbow and headroom for the expanding river traffic. Even this structure needed further improvements, forming the basis of the bridge that links the centres of Rochester and Strood today.

Early in the twentieth century shipbuilding came to an end at Sheerness Dockyard, but Chatham was still constructing fighting ships and in 1908 delivered the *C17*, a significant vessel, being the first of fifty-seven submarines to be built at the yard over the coming fifty-nine years. At the same time a factory at Eastchurch on the Isle of Sheppey was busy developing experimental aeroplanes. So successful were Short Brothers that in 1913 they moved to a more spacious home at Rochester Esplanade, just upstream from the bridge.

Thousands of floatplanes were produced from the new works for the 1914–18 conflict, but during the recession years of the 1920s Shorts built several sailing barges to keep themselves afloat. However, the company were to later achieve worldwide recognition through the production of the famous Sunderland flying boat, the first of which entered service in April 1938. After the war Shorts built eleven more flying boats, which were variants of the Sunderland, before closing their Rochester headquarters in July 1948 to move to Belfast.

Quiet times at Short Brothers' Rochester seaplane works: Rochester Castle *was one of several barges built by the company during periods of low demand for their flying craft.*

On the west side of the Medway estuary sits the Isle of Grain. It was here in 1923 that an ambitious American, Charles Ganahl, opened a small oil refinery. His enterprise, under the direction of the Medway Oil and Storage Company, was to last only nine years, although the installations remained in place throughout the Second World War, contributing to the famous Pluto pipeline, pumping petrol under the Channel to Allied Forces in Normandy. In July 1950, however, work began on the construction of Europe's largest refinery, commissioned by the Anglo-Iranian Oil Company (later the British Petroleum Company). Fully completed in March 1953 at a cost of £26 million, the refinery could berth the largest tankers of the day, although the massive supertankers of later years could only be handled part-loaded.

On the opposite side of the estuary, Sheerness Dockyard was eventually to fall victim to economic cuts placed upon the Royal Navy and was purchased in March 1960 as a trading estate. Just one day later it opened as a commercial port under the operation of the Medway Ports Authority. Sheerness became the main United Kingdom port for the first transatlantic LASH (Lighter Aboard Ship) service and a ferry port for passenger and freight services to Holland. After a difficult period in the early 1990s, Sheerness port was bought by the Mersey

Height of activity at BP's Isle of Grain refinery: six ocean tankers berthed at the jetties of the huge Medway complex, which closed after thirty years of operation. (Copyright BP plc)

Docks and Harbour Company, its current owners, in 1993. Since then Sheerness has become a premier port handling fresh produce, vehicles and forest products. A new £2 million forest products terminal was opened at No.1 Berth in 1997, whilst reclamation of Lappell Bank, immediately upstream from the port's main berths, means that 45,000 vehicles can be stored on a 200-acre site equipped with modern security systems.

The 1980s brought further important changes to Medway's shipping and port facilities. Defence cuts were still ongoing and in June 1981 the Government announced that Chatham Dockyard would be closed. Operations would be run down over the space of three years, but there were many tears as the dockyard gates closed for the last time on 31 March 1984, a farewell to more than four hundred years of Royal Naval connections. Without delay the dockyard was divided into three projects: a commercial port, which would be developed around No.3 Basin, a large housing and business scheme on St Mary's Island and around No.1 and No.2 Basins, and a working museum telling the story of Chatham Dockyard and naval life at sea within the historic area of the yard. All three projects have proved successful: the commercial section, now known as Chatham Docks, handles forest products and steel coil at its eight berths; Basins 1 and 2, integral parts of a development called Chatham Maritime, host visiting sailing ships, warships and preserved vessels, whilst Chatham Historic Dockyard, the museum portion, has received full heritage recognition.

During the same year as the Chatham Dockyard announcement, there was further despondency when BP closed their Isle of Grain refinery after thirty years of service. Many jobs were lost and it seemed that the sight of a huge ocean ship entering the Medway estuary would be a memory of the past. Yet once again there was good news, the saviour this time being tycoon Peter de Savory, whose company Highland Participants announced the redevelopment of the site into Britain's third largest container port. The first phase of work began in December 1988, but by the end of 1989 Highland Participants had been bought out by three of its employees, forming Maritime Transport Services, who were soon investing in the dredging of approach channels and the acquisition of modern container handling equipment. On 14 September 1990 Thamesport, as the new terminal was now called, was officially opened and by the end of the following year an extension jetty had been added.

The next few years were not plain sailing as prospective customers were reluctant to transfer their ships to Thamesport from competing UK and European container ports and in 1995 the terminal was bought by Rutland Trust plc, followed by a further change of ownership in February 1998 when Hutchinson International Port Holdings invested £112 million. Soon Thamesport was moving forward; today its six giant ship-to-shore gantry cranes can handle container ships capable of carrying more than 5,000 standard-sized twenty-foot equivalent units (TEU) and there are further plans for expansion. Already some of the world's biggest shipping companies use the port and the frequent movement of ships in and out of Sheerness means that the Medway estuary is once again alive with ocean-going shipping.

For much of my life I have lived within earshot of ships' sirens on the Medway and a clear morning allows me a glimpse of Rochester's timber wharves. Half a century ago, when importation of wood pulp for the paper industry was at a peak, the Port of Rochester provided several thousand jobs. As I write, though, plans are in hand for yet more housing, this time to be developed on land opposite the existing wharves. Whilst this would be a feature of ongoing riverside improvements stretching from Gillingham to Rochester and including the provision of pleasant open spaces and waterside pathways, eight-storey blocks of flats and twenty-four-hour working wharves would be a curious mix.

Changes to the Medway's riverbanks have already followed a similar trend to that within the Port of London, the subject of my previous book. Like the Thames, the Medway now

The many facets of a modern port: large specialist terminals positioned next to the deep-sea berths of Sheerness. Beyond the quaysides, thousands of new vehicles await distribution to UK outlets, whilst in the foreground is a ferry terminal at Garrison Point through which passengers would pass to and from their North Sea crossings.

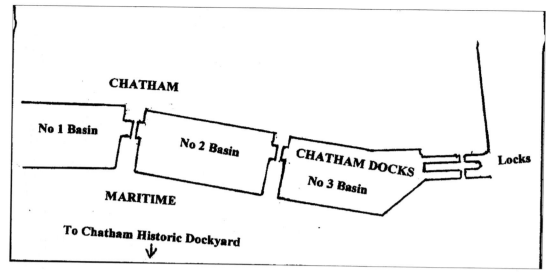

New docks for old: the three-basin system of the former Chatham naval base now comprises Chatham Docks, its commercial area and Chatham Maritime, a business and residential development around the remaining two basins, which host preserved craft, tall ships and warships.

sees little upriver commercial traffic, a variety of residential properties have sprung up where industries used to thrive and most ship-handling berths are now located downstream, in sight of the estuary.

Tidal Medway, from Allington Lock near Maidstone to its estuary, together with a further 5.6 nautical miles of water to the Medway Buoy in the Thames Estuary, are under the control of Medway Ports, based at Sheerness. Its jurisdiction extends for just over twenty-seven navigable miles in total, allowing for Chatham's enclosed docks, Queenborough Harbour on the Isle of Sheppey and Faversham and Milton Creeks on the River Swale. Like the port of Sheerness and Chatham Docks, Medway Ports is under the ownership of the Mersey Docks and Harbour Company.

Since my boyhood days, when I would venture with some trepidation along the creeking well-used piers of Chatham to watch pulp ships, barges and little tugs busy at work, the waters of the Medway have witnessed countless changes. I have been fortunate enough to observe and photograph the surprisingly wide variety of shipping which has used the river, examples of which are profiled over the coming pages, which I trust you will find interesting.

Like huge long-necked, four-legged creatures, container-handling cranes at Thamesport tower above visiting shipping.

The Medway's tidal waters are under the control of Medway Ports.

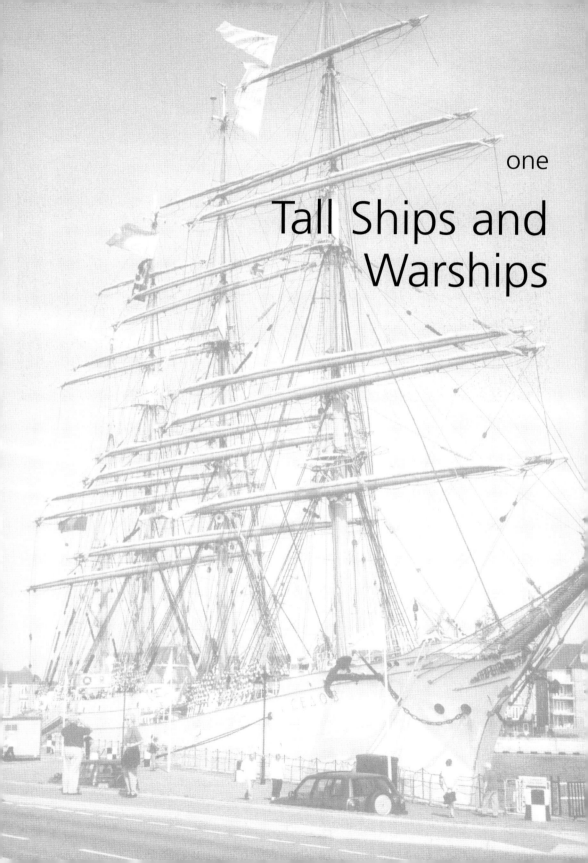

one

Tall Ships and Warships

King Henry VIII's decision to base his nation's fleet in the Medway was a turning point in the river's history, but he surely could not have envisaged that some five centuries later Chatham would still be attracting well-known sailing vessels and fighting ships. The popularity of holidays and training courses on tall ships encourages some of the most elegant vessels in the world to visit the former naval base, whilst Royal Naval vessels with local connections make courtesy calls, opening their doors the public.

Following the launch in 1646 of Chatham's first frigate, weighing just 315 tons, the Dockyard's slipways were constantly busy with bigger and more powerful constructions, culminating in a series of six Oberon-class submarines, the final three of which were built for the Canadian Navy between 1964 and 1967. Happily, the last Royal Naval submarine built at the yard – HMS *Ocelot* – has returned to her birthplace as one of Chatham's most popular attractions, a tribute to the Dockyard's expertise in submarine construction.

In 1928, Chatham Navy Days began its long successful run, which, apart for an interval for the Second World War, lasted until 1981. The event was re-launched in 1999 amidst a fanfare of optimism, with more than 100,000 people attending, but after two further years was discontinued. It remains to be seen whether the event will be revived for a second time, especially in this age of high instability across the world.

A ship with local connections – HMS Chatham.

The Russian sail-training vessel Kruzenshtern *berthed at No.2 Basin, Chatham Maritime, during a courtesy visit. The last deep-water, cargo-carrying sailing ship to be built, she was completed as the* Padua *for F. Laeisz of Hamburg. She was handed over to the USSR in 1946. She is 3,515grt, 114m x 14m and accommodates 168 cadets and sixty-eight men.*

High and mighty: the mainmast of Kruzenshtern *stands 50m tall.*

The Royal Naval cruiser Superb, 8,800 tons displacement, was one of the largest warships to grace Chatham Navy Days during the 1950s. Built by Swan Hunter, she was commissioned in November 1945 and broken up at Dalmuir in 1960.

Built at Chatham, moored at Strood: HMS Trenchant was a 'T'-class submarine, built for the Royal Navy in 1943. Displacing 1,571 tons, she sailed with a complement of fifty-nine officers and men. She was scrapped at Faslane in 1963.

A majestic memory: the training ship Arethusa *was moored off Lower Upnor for more than forty years. Built as the* Peking *at the Blohm & Voss shipyard in Hamburg, she sailed for the famous German Laeisz Line on worldwide cargo routes with her equally graceful sisters* Pamir, Parma *and* Passat. *As sail gave way to steam, she was purchased as a training ship and run by Shaftesbury Homes, becoming a home and school accommodating up to 240 boys wishing to pursue careers in the Royal and Merchant Navies. In 1975 she was sold to American interests and towed in 1977 to New York where she can be seen under her original name of* Peking *at the South Street Seaport Museum. Today a land-based facility at Lower Upnor, the Arethusa Venture Centre, offers residential courses in outdoor activities, sport and environmental education to children of primary school age.*

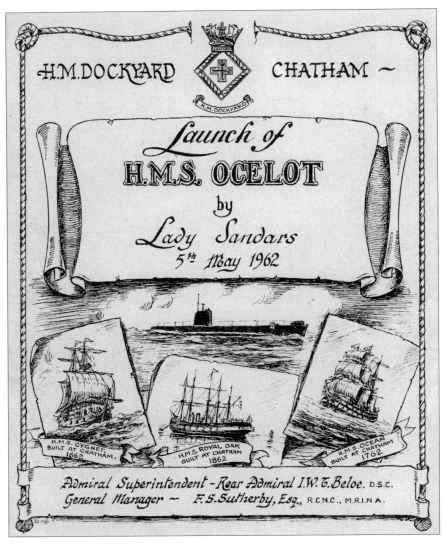

The official commemorative programme issued at the launch of HMS Ocelot, the last Royal Naval submarine built at Chatham Dockyard.

Opposite below: The three-masted barque Lord Nelson berthed at Chatham Historic Dockyard's Thunderbolt Pier in 1995. One of two vessels operated by the Jubilee Sailing Trust specifically to encourage the integration of able bodied and physically disabled adults through the medium of tall ship sailing. Her dimensions are: 368grt, length 55m, beam 9m, masthead height 33m. She has ten permanent crew, including a master and forty voyage crew, half of whom are disabled. She sails three- to ten-day voyages around the British Isles, Europe and the Canary Islands.

HMS Ocelot *in retirement, moored against the river wall at Chatham prior to entering her permanent dry-dock home. Commissioned on 31 January 1964, she operated with a complement of sixty-nine and had a range of 9,000 nautical miles at a 12-knot service speed, and a 1,610-tons standard displacement. Sold for breaking, she was saved by the Chatham Historic Dockyard Trust who purchased her for £90,000 and she arrived back at her birthplace on Sunday 12 July 1992.*

Above and below: *HMS* Cavalier *arriving at Chatham Historic Dockyard in May 1999 to start a new life as a static attraction. Built by J. Samuel White & Co., Cowes, she was launched on 7 April 1944 and completed on 22 November that year. She saw war action with the 6th Destroyer Flotilla and sailed worldwide before being laid up at Chatham in 1972. In 1977 she moved to Southampton, then to Brighton, then in 1987 to Hebburn, South Tyneside after which plans for her to be part of a museum were never realised and she was left languishing in dry dock. Happily, sufficient funds were raised to enable The HMS* Cavalier *(Chatham) Trust to bring their ship back to Chatham.*

Moored in the River Medway during one of her visits, Grand Turk *is a full-size replica of an eighteenth century twenty-two-gun frigate. Built at Marmaris in Turkey, she was launched in August 1997 and was employed as the central feature in the television series 'Hornblower'. She has twelve working sails and two diesel engines, and is 46.33m x 10.36m with a mainmast of height 35.66m. She is owned and was built by R.J. Turk & Sons who specialise in supplying craft for the film industry and who have moved from their Surrey base into the No.7 Slip at Chatham Historic Dockyard.*

Flying in front: the distinctive bows of the Dutch brigantine SwanFan Makkum, *which arrived for a Chatham Maritime event. Built in 1993, she is 62m long and her accommodation consists of eighteen double cabins.*

At her permanent home in No.2 Dry Dock, Chatham Historic Dockyard, HMS Cavalier *forms part of a three-ship 'Battle Ships' exhibition with HMS* Ocelot *and the nineteenth century sloop HMS* Gannett, *described overleaf, in adjacent dry docks.*

Home and dry: HMS Ocelot *is open to the public, as are the other two vessels in the exhibition.*

Home Port visit of
HMS CHATHAM
at Chatham Maritime
Programme of Events

**HMS Chatham will be open to the public
at Chatham Maritime in Basin No.2 on
Saturday 17 & Sunday 18 June 1995
between 10.00am - 5.00 pm**

A programme describes the visit of HMS Chatham to the former naval town after which she is named. During this event the ship was awarded the Freedom of the City of Rochester upon Medway.

Type-22 Frigate HMS Chatham manoeuvres in No.2 Basin, Chatham Maritime, during a more recent call. Commissioned at Chatham in May 1990, she is the seventh warship to bear the name. She has a complement of 237.

Work commencing: early days in the restoration of HMS Gannett in a Chatham Historic Dockyard dry dock. A Dotterel Class screw sloop, she was built at Sheerness Dockyard, where she was launched on 31 August 1878. Made of teak on iron frames and rigged as a barque, she is 1,130 tons displacement. In 1904 she became HMS President, headquarters of the London Division of the Royal Naval Voluntary Reserve. Later she was refitted as a training school and employed as HMS Mercury on the River Hamble from 1914–1968. She was then sold to Chatham Dockyard Trust; grants for her restoration have so far totalled £3 million.

Work progressing: with two shortened masts put in place, HMS Gannett returned to the waters of the Medway for a few weeks in 1999 whilst transferring to another dry dock.

Work completed: HMS Gannett *restored to her former glory in 2004 and featuring in Chatham's 'Battle Ships' exhibition.*

A general view of Chatham Navy Days 2000, featuring the largest warship in attendance, HMS Cumberland, *commissioned as the second of four Batch 3 Type-22 frigates in June 1989.*

The world's largest sailing ship, the four-masted full-rigged barque Sedov has twice graced the Medway since her first visit to Chatham Maritime in 1998. She was launched at Kiel in 1921 as Magdalene Vinnen, a clipper that would carry cargoes between Australia, Chile and Europe. Renamed Kommodore Johnsen in 1936, she became a Baltic training ship during the Second World War. Handed to the USSR in 1946, she was renamed Sedov. She is currently operated by the University of Murmansk for the Russian State Fishing Ministry as a sail-training vessel. She is 117.95m long and has a crew of seventy plus 130 merchant navy cadets.

Reflections of a fine ship: a bow view of Sedov, berthed in No.2 Basin, Chatham Maritime.

A ship with two careers, throughout both of which she had close Medway connections. The Antarctic ice patrol ship HMS Endurance *was completed in December 1956 as* Anita Dan, *a Danish cargo vessel that would frequently moor at Rochester (see profile in next chapter). Converted by Harland &Wolff, Belfast, 1967–68 when a helicopter extension was added, she re-entered service in her second role, still sporting a bright red hull but equipped with two helicopters and accommodation for 142 officers and crew. She measures 2,641grt. She was involved in the Falklands War of 1982 and received a great welcome when she arrived back at Chatham on 20 August that year. She was disposed of in 1991 to be replaced by a new* Endurance.

Hardly a tall ship, but a sailing ship of note which berthed at Chatham in 1996, Matthew *is a copy of the ship in which John Cabot set sail from Bristol to discover Newfoundland in 1497. Launched in 1995, she cost £1.3 million to build and weighs over eighty tons. In May 1997 she set out on a re-enactment of Cabot's long journey.*

The sweeping lines of a modern frigate: HMS Cumberland *displaces 4,600 tons, has a length of 148.1m, breadth of 14.8m and a complement of 259.*

HNLMS Tydeman, *an oceanographic research ship of the Royal Netherlands Navy sails into Chatham Maritime for Navy Days 2001. She measures 2,977 tons displacement, 90.2m x 14.4m and has a complement of sixty-two plus fifteen scientists.*

A life on the ocean wave: the Band of HM Royal Marines, Portsmouth, perform their repertoire alongside HMS Kent *berthed at Chatham in 2001.*

Another visit to Chatham by Grand Turk, *this time facing downriver as she lies at Thunderbolt Pier.*

1985 CUTTY SARK TALL SHIPS' RACE

MEDWAY 20-24 JULY 1985 · CUTTY SARK TALL SHIPS' RACE ·

"Largest 'Parade of Sail' Ever To Be Seen On The Medway"

The heading of an official pamphlet advertising the only occasion to date that contestants of the annual Tall Ships Race have sailed up the Medway.

The British brig Royalist *is an experienced Tall Ships' Race competitor. She was built 1971 and is operated by the British Sea Cadet Association. She is 29.57m long.*

A plaque on board Royalist *commemorates her naming by HRH Princess Anne in August 1971. At the time of this photograph the vessel was making a rare visit to Strood.*

The Ukrainian full-rigger Kersones, *2,284grt, displays her decorative squared-off stern whilst berthed in Chatham Maritime. Built at Gdansk, Poland, in 1989, she is a former Soviet sail trainer.*

An unlikely Medway resident over recent years has been a former Soviet submarine, moored off Strood Pier. Built in 1967, U-475 was a member of a large class of Foxtrot submarines that formed the bulk of the USSR's submarine force in the Mediterranean. She later saw service in the Baltic before decommissioning in 1994 following which she was displayed on the Thames at Woolwich, then as an attraction at Folkestone. Owned by International Management Consortium, she is 91.5m x 8m and when in service was 1,950 tons displacement surfaced, with a complement of seventy-five, and with a surface speed of 18 knots.

Twinned for the occasion: BNS Crocus, a Belgian Flower-class minehunter (foreground) with HNLMS Vlaardingen, a Netherlands class minehunter (behind).

Viewed from under the ornate bows of Sedov, *the Ukrainian full-rigger* Khersones *and, ahead of her,* Atlante, *a 30-metre yacht dating from 1961. All three vessels were visiting Chatham Maritime for a special tall ships event in 2002.*

Dressed overall, HMS Kent is star of the show at Chatham Navy Days 2001. The Type-23 frigate was launched on 27 May 1998 by HRH Princess Alexander of Kent and was the first ship of the twenty-first century to join the Royal Navy when commissioned two years later. She is 4,300 tons standard displacement and 133m x 15m.

HNLMS Dordrecht represented the Royal Netherlands Navy at Chatham Navy Days 2000. An Alkmaar-class minehunter, she was commissioned into service in November 1983. She is 595 tons displacement (full load) and 51.4m x 8.9m with a speed of 15 knots and a complement of up to forty-two.

two

Baltic, Short-sea and Coastal Cargo Ships

From the nineteenth century onwards, commercial shipping services into the Medway were developed around the requirements of the local industries. Once iron and steel had taken prevalence over wood in the art of shipbuilding, cement and paper manufacturing predominantly influenced the type of cargoes shipped into the river. Raw materials and finished products to and from the cement factories would normally be carried by small coasters, as would china clay for paper making, delivered direct to Reeds' Aylesford mill.

Scandinavian pulp bought by Reeds would be imported to Rochester by larger cargo ships, mooring midstream at Rochester buoys where they would discharge their cargoes into waiting lighters for towing upriver to the mill. This trade created the appearance in the river of vessels owned by Scandinavian-based companies such as Iris Redeerei of Sweden, O/Y Finnlines of Finland and J. Lauritzen, well-known Danish shipowners whose red-hulled ships would lighten up the most dreary Medway morning. British-flagged pale yellow cargo ships owned by F.T. Everard & Sons would augment the scene.

Port services associated with the handling of these ships and their cargoes were provided by local companies. Among these were Thomas Watson (Shipping) Ltd, the nominated agents and stevedores, and the London & Rochester Trading Company Ltd who carried out the lighterage work. Both companies were shipowners in their own right, operating dry cargo vessels and barges. Watson's were based at Rochester for some 120 years before closing for business in the year 2000, but London & Rochester became Crescent Shipping, part of the Hay's Group, whose modern fleet of vessels currently trade around the UK and into the Continent.

The wood pulp trade underwent notable changes in the 1970s with an increase in imported manufactured newsprint and the implementation of new safety measures concerning carriage of pulp by sea. A method of recycling used paper was under development by Reeds and by 1980 the trade into Rochester had virtually ceased.

Today, the Medway is an important hub for forest products imported into the UK and quantities of wood pulp are still brought in for use by paper manufacturers across other parts of Kent and in northern England and Scotland. Apart from the deep-sea port of Sheerness, forest products such as timber, plywood and wood pulp are handled at Crown Wharf and the nearby Scotline Terminal at Rochester, and in Chatham Docks, the commercial area of the former Royal Naval Dockyard. Another Chatham import is steel coil, shipped in by short-sea vessels that load scrap metal for their return journeys. A similar trade was maintained at Stanley's Wharf, Rochester, until the last decade.

The largest vessels to encroach the waters of the Medway beyond its estuary ports, are coal-carrying bulk carriers serving Kingsnorth Power Station. The most frequent callers are ships in the colours of EON, formerly Powergen, owners of the power station. These ships make on average three calls a week.

On the banks of the Medway at Hoo stand the offices of another local shipping company, Lapthorn Shipping Ltd. Founded in 1951 with the purchase of a barge, the *Nellie*, this family firm holds the accolade of owning the largest British-registered dry cargo fleet totalling, at the time of writing, eighteen short-sea vessels.

A scene that encapsulates everything about daily commercial life on the River Medway around the middle of the twentieth century. The Finnish cargo ship Finntrader *(1951/4,022grt), owned by O/Y Finnlines Ltd, is moored at Rochester buoys. Alongside her, lighters await further cargoes of wood pulp for transportation upriver to Reed's paper mill near Aylesford. Other small craft lie on the Medway mud until the next tide.* Finntrader *left the Baltic trade in 1970 on being sold and transferred to Liberian registry as* Triton Ambassador.

A ship with an interesting history and which served the Medway under two separate ownerships. Laura Dan *(1933/1,511grt) was Danish owned and operated under the management of J. Lauritzen until 1941 when she was interned in Uruguay and taken over by the Uruguayan government. She was chartered to the United States War Shipping Administration in 1942 and renamed* Rocha. *In 1945 she returned to her pre-war owners and her name reverted to* Laura Dan. *In 1960 she was acquired by Thomas Watson (Shipping) Ltd, Rochester, and renamed* Lady Sharon. *She was changed to Panamanian ownership in 1961, then sold to further Panamanian owners in 1963 and renamed* Tico. *She was broken up in Holland in 1966.*

Crescent Shipping's cargo vessel Luminence *(1977/1,595grt) undergoing a refit in a Chatham dry dock. She is 91.3m x 13.25m with two cargo holds and a service speed of 12 knots. She was sold to Adelfo Com Int Lda, Portugal in 1999 and renamed* Virtual.

At low tide: the little coaster Antiquity *(1933/311grt) was a typical fleet member of F.T. Everard & Sons, Greenhithe whose dry-cargo ships were regular visitors to the Medway and Thames. Sold by Everard's in 1966, she was converted to a sand dredger and renamed* Tay Merchant.

It's January 1963 and the big freeze has returned to the Medway. A crew member finds a method of traversing the frozen waters as he makes for the shores from the Swedish steamship Titan *(1947/1,832grt), moored at Rochester buoys. Owned by Iris Redeerei, the vessel was launched as* Wartum *and was formerly* Kindu *until 1951. In 1968 she was sold to Greek interests.*

Profiled in Chapter Two as the Antarctic ice patrol ship HMS Endurance following conversion in 1967–68, Anita Dan (1956/2,641grt) was an example of the red-hulled ships of J. Lauritzen which became familiar sights at Rochester buoys over the years. Built at Rensburg, she measured 91.13m x 14m and had a service speed of 14 knots.

Everard's largest dry-cargo ships were recognisable by their yellow hulls and funnels, rather than the black worn by smaller vessels in the fleet. Georgina V Everard, 2,536grt, joined the fleet in 1955. She measured 93.27m x 12.8m and had a speed of 10 knots. She was sold to Lebanese interests in 1978, becoming Myassa, *then* Myassar.

The first of two Thomas Watson vessels of the same name, Lady Sandra, 356grt, was completed for the Rochester company in 1958. In 1968 she was sold to Manche Shipping Ltd with Thos Watson as managers, and renamed Sorel. In 1976 she was sold to Panamanian owners and renamed Mala M. In 1980 she was sold to Dubai owners, renamed Nasim, then Venus and broken up in Pakistan 1988.

Another example of an Everard dry-cargo coaster, Ability, 881grt, was built in 1943. She measured 61.87m x 9.1m with a speed of 10 knots. She was sold to Panamanian owners in 1975 and became Eleni V.

Although never acquiring the Lady *prefix traditionally allocated to Thomas Watson ships,* Susan *(1957/484grt) was nevertheless managed by the Rochester company for five years. Completed as* Jan Brons *for Dutch owners, she went aground in March 1964 and became a constructional total loss. She was repaired, sold to George Bell (Chartering) Ltd, Irish Republic, and renamed* Susan. *She was sold to V. Nolan Ltd, Irish Republic, then to G.E. Gray & Sons (Shipping) with Thos Watson as managers. She was transferred to Liberian owners in 1973 and broke in half and sank in November 1973.*

Like Titan, *featured earlier,* Rigel *(1938/2,400grt) was typical of the cargo vessels owned by Swedish company Iris Redeerei, which would moor at Rochester buoys at the height of paper manufacturing at Reed's mill. The vessel was broken up in Sweden in 1963.*

Owned by Thomas Watson (Shipping) Ltd from 1968 to 1971, Lady Sorcha, *344grt, was built in 1960 as* Vendome *for Lockett Wilson Line, London. She was sold by the Rochester company to J.A. Osborne, Montserrat and sank in August 1975 following a collision whilst en route for Montserrat from Trinidad. She measured 45.27m x 7.52m.*

The single-hatch dry-cargo vessel Crescence, *493grt, was built for Crescent Shipping Ltd in 1982. She has a length of 50m, breadth 9.2m and a draught of 3.3m. She operates at a speed of 10 knots.*

Lady Sybilla, *349grt, was a member of the Thomas Watson fleet from 1959 to 1972. Completed for Dutch owners in 1952, she was re-engined in 1965 but sold on by Thos Watson to Seatruck Ltd, London as* Celtic Sea. *She was renamed* Sam Nor *in 1974 and* Helliar Holm *in 1975. In 1976 she was sold to Cypriot owners as* Dorami *and in 1978 to further Cypriot owners as* Kimon. *She sank in Beirut Harbour after being struck by rockets during hostilities late in 1978.*

Following the days when pulp ships would discharge their cargoes at Rochester buoys, short-sea cargo vessels such as the single-hatch Sagitta *(1990/998grt) have been handled at the port's riverside wharves.*

Steel Shuttle *(1985/993grt) and her identical sister* Steel Sprinter *ran a regular service between the Dutch port of Ijmuiden and Stanley's Wharf, Rochester, carrying steel coil until the closure of the wharf to short-sea trade in the last decade. Thereafter the ships called at Chatham Docks until being sold to Cypriot interests in 2001 and being renamed* Joanne *and* Jennifer, *respectively. They measured 64.78m x 11.1m.*

Owned by R. Lapthorn & Co., whose headquarters are on the banks of the Medway at Hoo, near Rochester, Hoo Finch *(1989/794grt) is a modern British coastal and short-sea dry-cargo vessel. She measures 58.27m in length and 9.5m wide.*

Sailing into the Port of Rochester is the Dutch-registered Flinterborg, *1,990grt. Built in 1999, she has a service speed of 11 knots and measures 82m x 12.6m.*

Another Thomas Watson ship was Lady Sanchia *(1950/1,438grt). Built in Bruges as* Alphonso *for Belgian owners, she was acquired by Thos Watson 1966. She was sold and renamed* Owenbawn *in 1968, and in 1976 she was sold and renamed* Alexandra K II. *In 1981 she was sold and renamed* Lara Diana *and in 1984 she was sold with a new name* Anaam. *She was demolished in 1985 at Tripoli.*

Swedish-flagged ships of Ahlmark Lines AB regularly call at Crown Wharf, Rochester, with their cargoes of forest products. Sommen, 4,426grt, has been one of the largest and most frequent users of the wharf for much of her career. Built at Shanghai in 1983 she measures 105.95m x 17.56m with a speed of 13.5 knots. She has been strengthened for heavy cargoes.

The low-draught cargo ship Rhine-Liner *arriving in Chatham Reach. Designed to negotiate European waterways many miles from the sea, at 2,319grt she was built at Emden in 1978 as* Rhone Liner. *She became* Smederevo *in 1981–82 and then* Rhone Liner *again until 1992 when she acquired her present name.*

The Dutch cargo vessel Lindeborg *(1982/3,222grt) berthed in the Port of Rochester. She measures 82.38m x 15.83m with a speed of 11.5 knots. Sold in 1996 and renamed* Linden, *she was sold again 1999. She is now named* Beluga Obsession *and registered in Antigua and Barbuda.*

Lord Hinton *(1986/14,201grt), one of a series of bulk carriers built for the Central Electricity Board in the 1980s discharges coal at Kingsnorth Power Station. She is seen here displaying the funnel colours of Powergen plc UK, the power station's owners. She measures 154.87m x 24.54m with four hatches and has a speed of 12.5 knots.*

Arianta, a member of the Shell UK coastal tanker fleet, in dry dock within the Chatham Historic Dockyard. Built in 1982 as Shell Technician, *she was renamed in 1993. She measures 1,926grt and 79.3m x 13.2m. She was sold to F.T. Everard 1999 and renamed* Activity.

The modern Dutch coaster Alissa, *1,143grt, sails down the Medway. Built in 1996, she is 81.4m long, 9.5m wide and is owned by Scheepvaartbedrijf de Haan.*

A busy day at Chatham Docks: wood pulp is lifted by a dockside crane from the hatch of the short-sea vessel Buxtehude.

Opposite above: *Steel coil is regularly shipped into Chatham Docks for local firm Kent Wire. The Dutch vessel* Marja *(1993/2,715grt) has discharged her cargo and is about to load scrap metal for her outward journey. Owned by Rederij Marja BV, she has a speed of 11 knots and can carry up to 197 TEU.*

Opposite below: Scot Ranger *(1997/2,260grt) unloads her cargo of timber at Scotline's Rochester terminal. The company has two other independent terminals at Goole and Inverness, its base port, and operates its fleet of eight ships between Varberg in Sweden, Baltic ports and Rochester, Goole and Ireland.*

The company Hanson Aggregrates operates a fleet of hopper/suction dredgers and also owns an aggregates wharf situated on the Frindsbury Peninsular opposite Chatham Historic Dockyard. At the wharf its vessel Arco Bourne discharges sand and gravel dredged from the seabed to a depth of up to 36m. She measures 3,329grt and 97.53m x 17.03m. She was built 1981 and was formerly named Cambourne until 1997.

Viewed from the opposite quayside of the dockyard No.3 Basin, which now constitutes Chatham Docks, the 2,565grt Buxtehude flies the flag of Cyprus. Built as Rita at Hamburg in 1985, she was renamed in 1995. She carries up to 153 TEU, is ice strengthened and has a speed of 11 knots.

Forest products terminal operator Convoys Ltd transferred its port facilities from Deptford on the River Thames to Chatham Docks in August 2000, having purchased Crescent Wharves from Hays plc. At one of its wharves, packaged timber is unloaded from the dry-cargo vessel Union Gem.

The Dutch cargo vessel Bornrif *(1996/1,882grt) berthed at a Rochester wharf. Owned by H. Schwink, she is strengthened for heavy cargoes and ice. She is capable of navigating Continental inland waterways.*

Built in 1991 as the British-flagged North Sea Trader, Union Gem, *2,230grt, is owned by Union Transport Ltd. She has two holds and can carry 114 TEU. Note her stern-facing lifeboat, which is a common feature on modern-day short-sea vessels.*

three

Ocean Tankers
and Freighters

TMM CAMPECHE

LONDON

In the years following the arrival of the first full load of crude oil from Kuwait in the BP tanker *British Skill* on 4 November 1952, the jetties of British Petroleum's Isle of Grain refinery were occupied by some of the world's largest and most modern ocean tankers. Ships of BP's substantial tanker fleet were frequently in evidence and by the end of the 1970s supertankers of up to 280,000 tons deadweight could berth at eight of the refinery's eleven jetties, just a year or two before the closure of the giant complex.

Across the Medway estuary at the developing port of Sheerness, 1969 heralded the first LASH (Lighter Aboard Ship) arrival when *Acadia Forest* sailed in from the United States. The service was extended over the next three years with the addition of two similar ships. The vessels would moor at a former battleship mooring just off Sheerness where their rectangular lighters would be discharged for towing to narrower, shallower waters.

Sheerness currently handles a variety of imported forest products, much of which is shipped in from South America by bulk carriers of the giant Gearbulk organisation, although areas as far afield as the Far East, Russia, Sweden, the USA and Canada are also important sources of production. Investment into a fresh fruit terminal has seen Sheerness become the United Kingdom's principal port for imported fresh produce with the latest techniques controlling the transportation of fresh fruit from ship to supermarket shelf. The port's biggest customer, Capespan, has a joint interest in the futuristic terminal, whilst Seatrade Reefer Chartering, who operates a worldwide fleet of 120 refrigerated cargo ships, has a regular liner service into Sheerness, as does Cool Carriers AB, a Swedish concern.

Vehicle carriers may resemble huge boxes at sea but they do a sterling job in bringing many thousands of new cars and trucks to the UK's shores. Sheerness has been receiving at least 400,000 vehicles each year, of which about half are Peugeot Citroëns. The ships can berth at any one of six roll-on–roll-off berths at the port, including specialist car berths close to an expansive vehicle storage area. Lines using Sheerness include the huge Wallenius Wilhelmsen group, and Nippon Yusen Kaisha (NYK) and Mitsui OSK Lines, both of Japan.

The rise in fortunes of Thamesport, constructed on the Isle of Grain following the closure of the BP refinery, has coincided with the attraction of increasing numbers of container shipping lines to its berths. The very first ship to arrive was the German feeder vessel *Frisia 1* (1972/999grt), followed in July 1990 by *Ville de Venus* (1988/18,037grt), which inaugurated a Far East service for her French owners. Since then the vast Evergreen Marine Corporation of Taiwan has become one of Thamesport's biggest clients after transferring its UK business from Felixstowe. Its ships are employed on round-the-world services, sailing in both easterly and westerly directions. Other significant lines attracted to Thamesport are Lykes Lines, Hapag-Lloyd, Neptune Orient Lines, NYK, and the rather laboriously named Compagnie Maritime d'Affrettement/Compagnie Generale Maritime, better known as CMA/CGM, following the merger of the two companies.

Immediately downriver from Thamesport a terminal owned by Foster Yeoman Limited receives quantities of granite shipped in by large self-discharging bulk carriers from Glensanda on the Scottish west coast. The Somerset-based company not only owns the Medway terminal, but also the specially-designed aggregate ships and the massive single granite quarry, the largest in the world, from which their cargoes are extracted. Most materials used in south-east England's civil engineering and construction industry, including the Channel Tunnel link, have arrived through the Foster Yeoman terminal.

The pride of the BP tanker fleet, British Queen, *32,187grt, arrives at the Isle of Grain refinery with assistance from two towage tugs of J.P. Knight, Rochester. Built at the John Brown shipyard, Clydebank, she was launched by Queen Elizabeth the Queen Mother on 17 September 1959 and delivered to BP three months later. Her deadweight tonnage was 53,383. She made more than fifty visits to the Kent refinery before being broken up at Kaohsiung in 1975. (Copyright BP plc)*

British Valour *(1957/22,681grt) was completed for BP in 1957. An average-sized ocean tanker of her day but tiny compared with the massive supertankers of later years, she measured 207.26m x 26.21m. She was sold to Transportes Intermar Armadora SA, Liberia in 1973 and renamed* Mesis. *She arrived for breaking up in Taiwan in October 1975.*

The first Lighter Aboard Ship (LASH) to arrive at Sheerness, Acadia Forest, *was joined by* Atlantic Forest *and* Bilderdyk, *pictured above, in 1972 to create a fortnightly service between New Orleans and the Medway port.* Bilderdyk, *35,826grt, was owned by Holland America Line and carried eighty-three barges. Measuring 261.4m x 32.2m, she was sold in 1986 and now sails as* Rhine Forest *for Forest Lines Inc.*

British Queen *crossing the oceans in 1963. Manned by a crew of seventy-six, her cargo space was divided into thirty-six tanks. Note her bridge superstructure placed separately amidships, a design trend in those days, unlike modern supertankers whose combined bridge and accommodation are positioned aft. (Copyright BP plc)*

At No.1 Berth, Sheerness, the Bangkok-registered bulk carrier Thor Alliance discharges her cargo of forest products. Equipped with five 25-ton cranes she measures 188.93m x 30.66m with five hatches. She can carry up to 1,000 TEU.

A modern palletised roll-on–roll-off (ro-ro) ship, Finnwood (2002/18,286grt) has arrived at Sheerness. Built at Gydnia, Poland, she is owned by B&N Finnwood Ltd, Sweden. She measures 158.6m x 25.6m. Note the large centre stern door/ramp.

Bulk carriers of the giant Gearbulk group maintain regular services between Brazil, Chile, Canada and the port of Sheerness, carrying forest products. A fleet member is Harefield *(1985/27,818grt), which can also carry grain and up to 1,584 TEU. She has seven hatches served by two large gantry cranes and measures 187.51m x 29.47m.*

Big does not always mean beautiful, as proved in this view of the vehicle carrier Morning Mercator *(1988/52,422grt) at Sheerness. She can accommodate 5,793 cars on her twelve decks. She measures 199.55m long and 32.47m moulded breadth. She was formerly named* HUAL Champ *until 2000, then* Auto Champ *and then* HUAL Tricorn *to 2003.*

The huge Taiwan-based Evergreen group became the second container-ship operator to choose Thamesport as its UK port of call, and the arrival of Ever Glowing *(1988/46,551grt) in January 1991 marked the beginning of this lucrative link, which still exists today. Built at Kaohsiung, the vessel has space for 3,428 TEU and measures 269.67m x 32.29m. She was sold in 2001 to Panamanian interests and renamed* Agios Dimitrios 1. *(Copyright Kent Messenger Group)*

Thamesport's modern cranes stand tall over the British container ship TMM Campeche, *35,958grt.Built in 1989, she can carry up to 3,032 TEU in her six cellular holds and on deck. She measures 240m x 32.21m and is owned by CPS No.1 Ltd. She was named* Choyang Park *until 2001.*

The 1991-built container ship Lykes Motivator *has already had a most varied career. Completed as CGM Pascal, she was renamed* Nedlloyd Pascal *in1995, became* CGM Pascal *again in 1998 and was renamed* Ville de Jupiter *and* Jupiter *in 2000, when she also acquired her present name. She is operated by Lykes Lines, Florida and can carry 2,690 TEU.*

Although not strictly regarded as an ocean freighter, the 4,115grt general cargo ship OPDR Sevilla *acts as a feeder container ship on this visit to Thamesport. Built in 1999, she carries 374 TEU in a single hold with two hatches. She measures 100.53m x 16.2m and is registered in Teneriffe.*

A white-hulled 'reefer' that serves Sheerness, Vermont Universal *(1987/7,286grt), is owned by Metrostar Marine Co. She measures 144.51m x 19.84m and is equipped with eight 5-ton derricks. She was named* Fortune Reefer *until 1996.*

One of Foster Yeoman's huge bulk carriers offloads granite shipped from Glensanda at the company's Medway terminal. The 55,695grt Yeoman Bridge and Yeoman Bontropp are recognised as the world's largest gravity-fed belt self-unloaders. Both built in Japan in 1991, they each measure 249.9m x 38.07m with five holds and ten hatches. They have a service speed of 15 knots.

Foster Yeoman's biggest bulk carriers are capable of discharging cargoes of granite at up to 6,000 tons per hour.

Four 19-ton cranes dominate the main deck of the 8,945grt refrigerated cargo vessel Packer. *Built in Spain in 1990, she is owned by Yaoki Shipping SA. She measures 141m x 22.33m and has a service speed of 20 knots.*

Loaded and ready to sail: another view of Lykes Motivator, *about to leave Thamesport with virtually a full complement of containers. She operates at a speed of just under 22 knots.*

Well, how do these huge container ships and their piles of boxes manage to negotiate the angry seas of the world?

five

Passenger Ships, Large and Small

With its sheltered position and close proximity to the piers of the River Thames and Kent coastal resorts, the Medway has long been an ideal waterway on which to while away a few gentle hours on a pleasure steamer. Records show that the first river excursions on the Medway were made in 1815 by the little steamer *Hope*. Over a century later, in 1919, the New Medway Steam Packet Company was formed, creating a long-standing tradition of busy summer seasons with the introduction of its most famous steamer, *Medway Queen,* in 1924. Sadly this once proud vessel now sits in a Medway creek, awaiting her fairy godmother to save her from oblivion. Paddle steamer trips can, however, be enjoyed on the busy little coal-burner *Kingswear Castle*, a former River Dart excursion vessel.

A ferry service between Sheerness and Vlissingen (Flushing) by a company called Olau Line (derived from the name of its founder Ole Lauritzen) was initiated in November 1974 by a chartered Norwegian vessel *Basto V.* Over subsequent years the service developed into a highly successful passenger ferry business with the launching of two 15,000-ton vessels *Olau Hollandia* and *Olau Britannia* in 1980 and 1981, later to be replaced by two much larger and more luxurious ships of the same names in 1989 and 1990.

As demand for passenger berths increased, a new £8.5 million terminal was built at Garrison Point, a forty-eight-metre linkspan being added to improve ship and passenger handling.

Yet, in May 1994, the town of Sheerness was shaken by the sudden announcement that the ferry service would close. Passenger figures had shown a slight downturn, but reports indicate that a seamen's dispute led to Olau's decision to pull out of Sheerness, so ending a ten-day strike by crew members of *Olau Hollandia*.

A replacement ferry service operated by Eurolink was introduced in May 1995, using two chartered vessels, renamed *Euromantique* and *Euromagique,* but disappointing passenger numbers resulted in the withdrawal of the service inside two years.

In the early 1990s there was an attempt to make Sheerness a UK port of call for cruise ships. The venture was supported by Cunard, but the lack of a passenger terminal at any of the port's deep-sea berths hardly helped its cause and the berths have subsequently been used solely by cargo-carrying vessels.

The Cunard cruise ship Vistafjord (1973/24,492grt) makes a magnificent sight as she approaches Garrison Point in the summer of 1992. During the early 1990s this classically designed vessel made a handful of calls at Sheerness, but subsequently transferred to Southampton as her UK base port.

A helping hand: a line from Vistafjord is taken by an assisting Medway tug.

Many tales have happy endings, but the story so far of the former River Medway paddle steamer Medway Queen *has shown little sign of finishing that way. Built at Troon in 1924 for the New Medway Steam Packet Co. Ltd, Rochester, she would ply regular summer seasons between Strood, Chatham, Sheerness and Southend, also serving Herne Bay and Margate, and, in later years, Clacton. She became a Second World War hero, evacuating 7,000 servicemen from Dunkirk on seven brave voyages. Her last commercial voyage was from Strood Pier on 8 September 1963. She was sold to Fortes Ltd in 1964 for use as a floating hotel. She was then consigned to the scrapyard in 1965 but saved by a syndicate who bought her for £60,000 and opened her as a floating nightclub on the Isle of Wight, where she was laid up after the venture failed. Brought back to Chatham on Easter Day 1984, her new owners, the* Medway Queen *Preservation Company are still fighting an uphill battle to keep her in restorable order at her current berth at Damhead Creek, near Kingsnorth Power Station. Their aim is to return her to her original condition, but it remains a mystery why they are struggling to attain sufficient funds, whilst ships with far less honourable careers have received large heritage grants.*

Medway Queen *makes her way upriver towards Strood Pier. This photograph would have been taken early or late in a summer season, for in the background the General Steam Navigation pleasure steamer* Queen of the Channel *can be detected in her usual winter lay-up berth at Rochester.*

Converted to a nightclub and restaurant, the third vessel to bear the name Rochester Queen *is moored at Rochester Pier. Built in 1935 she sailed as the Scarborough pleasure steamer* Coronia *until the Second World War, during which she gave service at the Normandy landings. Returning to Scarborough after the war, she was based at Poole, Dorset in 1968–1974 as* Bournemouth Queen. *As* Queen of Scots *she was a contractors vessel on the Clyde until 1982 when she arrived at Rochester with added accommodation.*

Built in 1961 at Port Glasgow as a tug for the Clyde Port Authority, the Clyde *was converted to an excursion vessel and operated on the Medway for a few years during the 1980s and 90s, linking Strood Pier, Chatham's Sun Pier and Southend during the summer season. Owned locally by Invicta Line Cruises, she carried sixty-five passengers. After the company folded, the vessel was seen in dilapidated condition, laid up in a dock at Las Palmas.*

Queen of the Channel *makes good headway during one of her many summer excursions. Built in 1949, this 1,475grt motorship was employed on cross Channel trips from Thanet resorts and occasional sailings from London. She operated alongside the older* Royal Daffodil *and near-sister* Royal Sovereign. *As well as her winter breaks at Rochester, she was laid up in the Medway following withdrawal from service after the 1966 season until being bought for service in the Greek Islands in 1968. She was renamed* Oia, *then* Leto *in 1976 and broken up at Eleusis 1984.*

In addition to Clyde *(left), Inivicta Line Cruises ran a river-bus service between Strood, Rochester and Chatham, employing* Clairest, *a former Norfolk Broads cruiser, carrying fifty-four passengers.*

For another Medway 'paddler' it has been a far happier story. The *94grt* Kingswear Castle *is currently the only fully operational excursion steamer based on the Kent river. One of three sisters, she was built in 1924 by Philip & Son, Dartmouth, for summer service on the River Dart, even inheriting the main engine of a 1904 paddle steamer of the same name. On retirement in 1965 she was bought by The Paddle Steamer Preservation Society, but initial lack of funds saw her moved to the Isle of Wight, where, like the* Medway Queen, *she was neglected. But she was much luckier and, following complete restoration, has been operating summer seasons on the Medway since 1985. She has a length of 34.7m, overall beam of 8.5m and is coal fired with a normal speed of 8 knots. She is certified to carry 235 passengers on river cruises, 100 elsewhere.*

Shining examples: positioned below the bridge and in pristine condition, the ship's bell of Kingswear Castle *and her builder's plaque dating back more than eighty years.*

A careful manoeuvre: Vistafjord *arrives at a Sheerness cargo berth during her brief programme of cruises from the port. Providing assistance are the Medway towage tugs* Lady Brenda *and* Lady Morag. *Delivered to the Norwegian America Line in 1973, the liner was managed by Norwegian America Cruises from 1980 before being sold to Cunard in May 1983 who renamed her* Caronia *in 1999. She was sold to the Saga Group to commence cruising in 2005 as* Saga Ruby.

A close-up study of Vistafjord*'s handsome profile.*

Medway Queen *takes a well-earned break. Measuring 316grt, she could carry up to 887 passengers on her summer day trips. Built with a coal-fired boiler, she was converted to oil burning in 1938, giving her a speed of around 12 knots. She measures 54.85m x 15.24m over her paddle frames.*

As part of the restoration work on Medway Queen, *apprentices from Devon-based Appledore Shipbuilders re-fabricated the vessel's funnel, combining traditional and modern skills. The rebuilt funnel was placed at a temporary home in Chatham Historic Dockyard in June 2002.*

Passing sisters: the 33,336grt luxury ferries Olau Hollandia *and* Olau Britannia, *introduced on the Sheerness–Vlissingen route to meet spiralling demand. Built at Bremerhaven, they entered service in September 1989 and May 1990, respectively, as replacements for two 15,000-ton ships of the same names. They have accommodation for 1,600 passengers and 575 cars or 118 trailers and measure 161m x 29m. Following Olau Line's withdrawal from Sheerness, the ships were chartered by P&O,* Olau Hollandia *becoming* Pride of Le Havre *and her sister being renamed* Pride of Portsmouth, *but 2005 sees them being taken over by Brittany Ferries following P&O's fleet reductions.*

Her decks devoid of passengers, Kingswear Castle *returns to her base at Chatham's Thunderbolt Pier after a winter overhaul.*

A view from the beach: Olau Line's ferry Olau Hollandia *at the extended Garrison Point terminal, Sheerness.*

The vintage paddle steamer Kingswear Castle *has proved popular with people of all ages.*

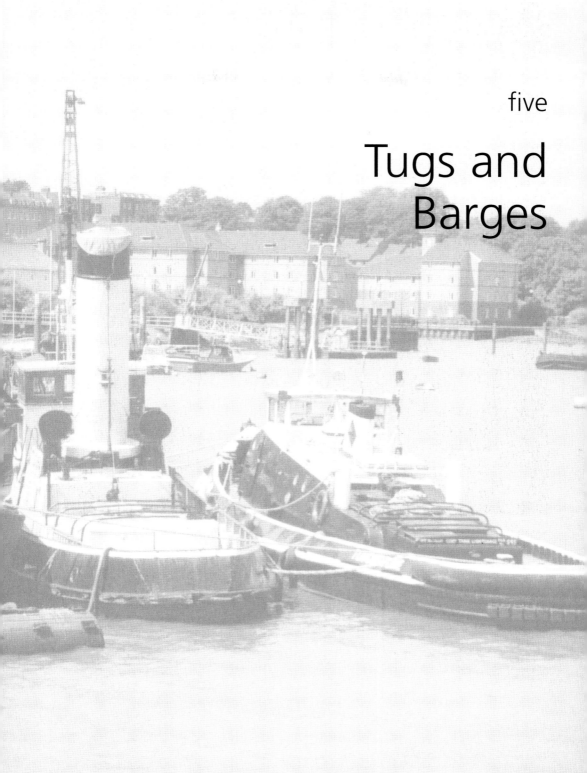

five

Tugs and Barges

The towage of ships, barges, lighters and anything else which could be moved on the River Medway was undertaken for generations by local tug company J.P. Knight. Instantly recognizable by their distinctive 'K' funnel emblem, its tugs became an integral part of the Medway scene over the years. Founded as the Kaiser Steam Tug Company in 1892, the firm prudently changed its name to J.P. Knight in 1914, benefiting handsomely from an upturn in trade after the First World War. In 1950, Knight's secured a thirty-year towage contract with BP's Isle of Grain refinery, later commissioning larger and more powerful tugs as the size of ocean tankers increased.

In 1991, the company's Medway towage business became part of the giant Howard Smith group, an Australian concern, later to be taken over by Adsteam, another Australian organization. Four modern tugs are now employed in Medway ship towage, primarily at Thamesport and Sheerness, under the control of Adsteam Medway. J.P. Knight have faithfully retained their headquarters within the Medway Towns but now concentrate on international towage and barge work in Scotland and as far away as South America.

Other Medway towage duties are under the care of Strood-based A.C. Bennett & Sons whose tugs and barges are seen additionally on the Thames. The company is currently involved in two major contracts: the distribution by barge of granite from Foster Yeoman's Isle of Grain terminal and the movement of barges filled with bulk rice imported from the United States and brought to Sheerness via Rotterdam by Lighter Aboard Ship. The rice barges are then towed up the Thames or to the riverside mill of Veetee Rice Limited, located on the industrial Frindsbury peninsular opposite Chatham Historic Dockyard.

Three to four decades ago there was a flurry of activity in the motor barge business with the delivery of almost twenty of these little vessels in the colours of the London & Rochester Trading Company. The majority were directly owned by the Strood-based company, but a few, although managed by London & Rochester, were under private ownership. They soon became familiar Medway characters, working alongside London & Rochester's fleet of ingeniously named tugs, *Shovette*, *Dragette*, *Lashette*…the theme continued, though, like the motor barges, their numbers depleted over the years with those remaining coming under the operation of Crescent Shipping.

Proudly displaying the funnel markings of local tug company J.P. Knight & Sons, for whom she was built in 1948, the 121grt Kent lies mothballed off Chatham Historic Dockyard as she awaits restoration. Employed as a duty tug at the Isle of Grain refinery for many years, she had the distinction of leading in the very first tanker to berth there – the British Skill – in 1950. Laid up from 1983, she was sold for just £1 to the South East Tug Society, who faithfully restored her to her original condition.

A good many small motor barges, some of which were constructed at Strood, have been owned by the London & Rochester Trading Co., later Crescent Shipping, over the years. One of these is Locator, 200grt, which still works on the Medway. She was built at Hull in 1970.

Tugs of Strood company Alan C. Bennett & Sons are employed in towing LASH barges loaded with rice to privately owned wharves on the Medway and Thames. The barges have originally come from the United States, transported to Rotterdam by a mother ship from where they are brought to Sheerness by a feeder ship, the Spruce. Here, the Bennett tug Sea Challenge II *(1969/85grt), formerly* Eduard, *is moored at the Veetee rice mill on the Frindsbury Pensinsular.*

The crew of the Medway-based tug Lady Morag *(1985/360grt) ex-*Kestrel, *set off on another mission from Sheerness. Like all modern 'tractor' tugs, their vessel is highly manoeuvrable, having the ability to be moved in virtually any direction at the flick of a joystick.*

Gently does it: Lady Morag *noses the cruise ship* Vistafjord *towards her Sheerness berth.*

At her new Medway home, St Mawes *(1960/120grt) was once the Thames towage tug* Ionia. *Sold to Falmouth Towing Company in 1987, she was renamed a year later and arrived in the Medway in 2003.*

Another job for Lady Morag, *this time carefully nudging the stern of a modern refrigerated cargo ship at a Sheerness quayside. The tug was owned by J.P. Knight, Rochester, until 1991 and is now operated by Adsteam Medway.*

Lady Emma II, *pictured at Chatham Maritime, displays the colours of Howard Smith Towage. Built in the Far East as* Chek Chau *in 1998, the 267grt tug arrived in the Medway later that year.*

Built in 1946, TID 172, a stern-driven harbour tug, spent much of her working life at Chatham Dockyard before being leased to the Netherlands Navy. After two years she returned to Britain to be sold for preservation. Now based in Essex she has revisited Chatham on several occasions as a fully operational tug.

Two preserved tugs moored at Chatham: left is TID 156, a wartime-built steam tug and right is Touchstone, a 68grt motor tug built in 1963 for Wm Cory & Son who sold her for only £1 to a Medway marine engineer. During her career she would have operated on the Medway as far upstream as Maidstone.

A waiting duo: moored near Sheerness are the Adsteam Medway tug Lady Brenda *(1985/360grt) formerly* Kenley *of J.P. Knight, Rochester, until 1991(left) and* Kinross *(1978/347grt), ex-*Fuji Maru *until 1981,owned by J.P. Knight (Caledonian) Ltd for whom she normally works in Scotland.*

The busy Lady Morag *has ventured upriver to Chatham Maritime for this job, assisting the Royal Naval destroyer* HMS Chatham *in No.2 Basin.*

Built at Rochester in 1965 the 172grt motor barge Francesca Prior *operated for many years as the* Roffen. *Owned by Capt. Alan Jenner, she was sold to J.J. Prior, for whom she had been on long-term charter, and following a rebuild at the Acorn Shipyard, Rochester, she re-entered service under her new name in 2003 with Capt. Jenner in command. She measures 29.2m x 6.7m.*

Lady Emma II positioned at Garrison Point, Sheerness in 2004. By now she has acquired the funnel logo of the Adsteam group who took over Howard Smith Towage and are responsible for large ship towage in the Medway.

Based at Chatham, TID 164, a steam tug built during the Second World War, has been successfully maintained in operational condition by a small preservation group. Like TID 156 and TID 172 featured earlier, she is one of 182 'TID' tugs built for the Ministry of War Transport between 1943 and 1946 and assembled at the Hessle and Thorne shipyards of Richard Dunston. She measures 19.81m x 5.2m.

six

Miscellaneous Ships

Ocean ships, coastal ships; restored ships, converted ships…the surprising diversity of shipping using the Medway is demonstrated within this chapter. Vessels making courtesy calls, others providing education and training, some just seeking safe moorings: the Medway welcomes them all.

Known since 1982 as the pirate radio station Radio Caroline, Ross Revenge (1960/963grt) was built at Bremerhaven as an Icelandic trawler, the Freyr. Sold to the Ross Group in 1963, she acquired her present name and was based at Grimsby. She had capacity for 300 tons of fish. She measures 70.1m x 11.6m and has an operational speed of 16 knots. After her purchase by Radio Caroline she was equipped with a 91m transmission aerial, which collapsed in the UK hurricane of 1987. In 1991 she was dry-docked in Chatham after running aground. Moored in the Medway at Chatham and Strood in the late 1990s, she returned to Strood in 2004.

Resting on the low tide mud, the Will *is the sole survivor of four steel-hulled spritsail barges built 1925–26 for F.T. Everard & Sons. Originally named* Will Everard, *she would carry cargoes into the Medway, as well as along the Thames. Sold in 1967, she was owned privately before the P&O group employed her in sales promotion and hospitality work. In 1999 she was taken over by Sue Harrison, her skipper for many years.*

Owned by UMD City of London Ltd, two self-discharging sand dredgers, carrying aggregates from designated banks in the North Sea and English Channel, make occasional calls into Chatham Docks in addition to their more regular voyages up the Thames to Charlton. City of Westminster *(1990/3,914grt), pictured above, and* City of London *(1990/3,660grt) each have a length of 99.8m.*

Moored adjacent to a variety of small river craft at Chatham, HMS Crysanthemum, *built in 1918 as an Anchusa-type 'Q' sloop, spent several years at various Medway locations before meeting her fate at a Strood scrapyard. A ship with an unusual history, she was used as a target towing and photographic ship after the First World War, then converted into a signals training ship in 1938. She even appeared in the film 'Indiana Jones and the Last Crusade'. Under the ownership of the Inter-Action Trust, she was berthed at London's Embankment for many years before arriving in the Medway awaiting sale. On 13 June 1995 she caught fire and was subsequently broken up. She was 1,290 tons displacement and 77.72m long.*

Opposite above: *The world's last operational Liberty ship,* Jeremiah O'Brien *brings back memories for many ex-seamen as she steams up the River Medway on 8 June 1994. Her visit to Chatham and other UK ports was the culmination of her first trans-Atlantic crossing since 1944, leaving her San Francisco home to participate in the 50th D-Day Anniversary celebrations. In addition to Chatham, she was open to the public at Portsmouth, Southampton and London.*

Opposite below: *Now a resident at Chatham Maritime, apart from when she is running educational trips, the former Port of London Authority launch* Havengore *will always be remembered for carrying the coffin of Sir Winston Churchill along the Thames during his state funeral in 1965. Restored by the Havengore Trust, by whom she was purchased from the PLA in 1995, she accommodates up to ten students studying modern history.*

In 1756 a Mr Jonas Hanway founded the Marine Society to encourage men and boys to join the Royal Navy. Since those days the Society has trained many thousands more for careers in both the Royal Navy and the Merchant Navy and currently operates two ships, Jonas Hanway, named after the founder, and Earl of Romney (seen here). Both vessels are frequently seen in the Medway, moored off Chatham Historic Dockyard or at Strood Pier. Formerly the 'E' Class inshore survey vessels HMS Egeria and HMS Echo, respectively, Jonas Hanway was taken on loan from the Ministry of Defence in 1986 whilst Earl of Romney was purchased outright in 1988. Both are 154grt and 32.6m x 6.7m. They have a crew of seven officers/instructors and twelve trainees.

Opposite above: *Another view of HMS* Crysanthemum, *having been moved to a mooring off Strood Pier, where she remained for five years. Each of her decks had been fitted out with teaching rooms and offices and these were still in evidence until the end of her days.*

Opposite below: Jeremiah O'Brien *is guided towards the lock gates of Chatham Maritime by the Crescent tug* Lashette.

Ross Revenge (Radio Caroline) off Acorn Wharf, Strood, her last Medway mooring to date, shortly before being moved to the Thames.

As if to emphasise the wide variety of craft using the River Medway, Earl of Romney *has positioned herself amongst boats of all shapes and sizes in Chatham Reach, including a retired lifeboat in the foreground.*

To dispel any doubts as to her identity, a banner is attached to the starboard side of Jeremiah O'Brien.

With a protective awning over her aft deck, Havengore *passes a winter's day at her berth in Chatham Maritime's No.1 Basin.*

A unique vessel, which was based at Chatham around the middle of the last decade, Ocean Defender, *200grt, owned by Earthkind of London, specialises in the rescuing and treating of marine animals and birds. Built at Oslo in 1912 as the* Berk, *a steam whale-catcher equipped with auxiliary sails, she escaped Nazi-occupied Norway and was used as a minesweeper by the Allies. She was later refitted as a trawler, then used as a short-sea trader before arriving in England for use as a pleasure boat, when she was purchased by Earthkind. She has a crew of seven: three professional and four volunteer scientists. (Copyright Kent Messenger Group)*

Along the Riverbank

Quiet towpaths, partially muddied by recent rain; overhanging willows, swaying gently above their own reflections in the calm water: the painted picture at Allington Lock, the upriver tidal limit of the Medway, contrasts completely with the busy modern port facilities of the river's estuary, some twenty-one miles downstream. Only the occasional passing white cabin cruiser and the sound of happy chatter from a nearby inn interrupt the tranquillity of this picturesque stretch of the Medway along which busy little tugs would tow lighters to Maidstone and Tonbridge a few decades ago. The peaceful scene continues to medieval Aylesford Bridge, just under a mile downstream, which would have proved quite an obstacle for the tugs and other small river craft, requiring them to lower their gear in order to negotiate the bridge's ten metres of headroom.

Industry quickly prevails over countryside as the Medway enters a wide chalk valley known as the Medway Gap. The intense filth of yesteryear, when a multitude of chimneys lined the riverbanks, is long gone, although emissions do rise from the few remaining paper and cement factories at Aylesford's industrial area and the small towns of Snodland and Halling.

The fine Medway Bridge, which receives fewer accolades than it deserves, originates from 1962, but now consists of three separate structures, carrying the M2 motorway in both directions and the Channel Tunnel rail link. In this vicinity are the first of several marinas, which provide good berthing facilities for the Medway's considerable population of private boats.

As Rochester Bridge comes into sight, modern residential properties line the Medway's eastern bank where Short Brothers and, in subsequent years, a number of industrial companies provided much-needed employment for the area. The recently restructured Rochester Pier is used by the paddle steamer *Kingswear Castle* for upriver trips. Beyond the bridge vessels of various shapes and sizes moor off Strood Pier, but no longer to discharge cargoes. Since the very first Medway excursion ships, the pier has been the starting point for many a jaunt down the river.

The unglamorously named Gas House Point, where port facilities are due to surrender to more housing, marks the beginning of a large reverse 'S'-bend in the river, incorporating Limehouse Reach and Chatham Ness, and leading into Chatham Reach. The main insertion is the Frindsbury Peninsular, once full of limekilns – hence the 'Limehouse' connection – but now a sprawling business park. Opposite the Peninsular, Ship Pier and the long-disappeared Blue Boar Pier were once the landing places for crewmen arriving from pulp vessels moored at Rochester buoys. Nearby public houses, now much more respectable, were reputed for their rather unsavoury characters in those days.

Chatham's Sun Pier is a good vantage point for Medway upriver shipping and was a regular landing stage for paddle steamers until 1959. In Chatham Reach the Medway passes the Chatham offices of Lloyd's of London, the famous insurance market through which most of the world's shipping fleets seem to be insured. Interest is maintained with the impressive sight of the covered slipways of the former Chatham Dockyard, currently housing exhibitions of historic interest, although the largest of them all – No.7 Slip – is inhabited by a firm of specialist builders of ships for the film industry. After almost forty years, shipbuilding, though on a smaller scale, has at last returned to Chatham!

The River Medway flows over its lowest crossing – the Medway Tunnel – before passing Upnor Castle, which houses an interactive recreation of the Dutch raid, and the picturesque waterfront of Lower Upnor with its inns, boathouses and land-based Arethusa Venture Centre.

Just downstream the grey-slabbed Napoleonic Hoo and Darnett Forts offer a grim reminder of the days when additional protection of Chatham and its Dockyard was required.

So far, on this downriver journey, numerous modern riverside developments have been observed: pleasant riverbank walks, for instance; a complete leisure park complex near Gillingham, known as the Strand; and balconied residential properties constructed on St Mary's Island, once a vital extension to the old Chatham naval base. Now the Medway enters a region of marshes and saltings, a narrow channel in Otterham Creek allowing access to Otterham Quay, which has been handling small coasters for years. The Medway widens in Long Reach where the largest vessels to encroach the river thus far tie up at the jetty of Kingsnorth Power Station.

After the lonely but lengthy Oakham Ness Jetty, used for pumping oil ashore for Kingsnorth, the river flows north-east through Kethole Reach, the scene of a terrible First World War tragedy. It was here that, on 27 May 1915, the Canadian Pacific liner *Princess Irene,* converted for war as a minelayer and stashed with some five hundred mines, blew up, killing 170 of her men.

Yet this loss of life was considerably smaller than experienced just seven months earlier during the HMS *Bulwark* disaster, a matter of metres downstream. The 15,000-ton battleship was anchored in the company of other members of the British fleet when she suffered a huge explosion, causing the loss of 727 of her 741 crew. Today, two buoys poignantly mark the position of her submerged remnants.

As the Medway Estuary comes into sight, modern technology at Thamesport towers over loaded container ships with the Isle of Grain Power Station beyond. To starboard the River Swale, which separates the Isle of Sheppey from the rest of Kent, receives shipping movements bound for Ridham Dock, which comes under the auspices of Medway Ports Authority and receives up to 800,000 tonnes of cargo each year, including timber, steel, fertilisers, grain and calcium carbonate slurry for papermaking at nearby Sittingbourne. The heavily employed quaysides of Sheerness port are now in view, the former passenger ferry linkspan at Garrison Point protruding like a solitary finger towards the Thames shipping lanes.

The Medway is among the United Kingdom's ten busiest arteries and never fails to interest shiplovers, historians and conservationists alike. There are almost ninety different marine facilities, from large terminals and wharves to upriver yacht clubs and moorings. Ancient buildings are full of tales from years gone by, whilst creeks and backwaters, seasonally populated with marine bird life, hold on to their own little secrets. During summer weekends large commercial vessels share the Medway's waters with thousands of leisure users, a fine balancing act, according to Medway Ports, but one which successfully blends the river's commercial and leisure interests. The Medway has seen many changes; indeed it is constantly changing. There is hearsay that a bridge may be constructed over the river at Chatham, which is causing concern for Rochester's wharf operators as it would prevent cargo ships from accessing the Port of Rochester. This apart, though, a continuing upward trend of shipping movements on the Medway means that there should be much optimism for the river's future.

An idyllic setting: the medieval stone bridge at Aylesford, watched over by the village church. When built, the bridge had eight arches, but these were gradually reduced to five (the far left arch is hidden by foliage) in order to aid navigation by river craft.

Where the Medway's tidal and upriver waters meet: Allington Lock originates from 1792 but is equipped with modern electrical sluices nowadays.

Located near a pronounced 'U'-bend in the River Medway, a paper mill dominates the area around Snodland just as it did when Mr Townsend and Mr Hook moved in around a century-and-a-half ago.

Back to Allington Lock where a renovated sailing barge fronts this picturesque scene.

Within a green valley in the Medway Gap, a large cement works still exists on the riverbank at Halling.

All types of small craft populate one of the Medway's marinas within sight of the Medway Bridge.

Medway Bridge, extended to three structures, allows 36m of headroom over the river.

Opposite above: *The former pleasure steamer* Rochester Queen *has moved from Rochester Pier to a permanent mooring at Port Medway Marina, Cuxton, where she operates successfully as a floating restaurant under new ownership.*

Opposite below: *Despite an influx of modern apartments on Rochester Esplanade, evidence still remains from the days when seaplanes and river barges were launched from the slipways of Short Bros.*

Standing tall over the Medway: Rochester's Cathedral and Castle. Before them (right) is moored Rochester Queen, *converted to a nightclub and restaurant, before being moved to her present home at a Cuxton Marina.*

Reconstructed and extended in 1998, Rochester Pier is used principally by the paddle steamer Kingswear Castle. *Close by are berthing facilities for private craft.*

Like Medway Bridge, the present Rochester Bridge comprises three structures. Furthest upriver, the Victorian road bridge was rebuilt in 1914 with steel bow-girders. A centre bridge was completed in 1971 to take eastbound traffic. Below the bridges there is a 5.5m difference between low and high tide.

Viewed from Bridge Reach, the lattice girders of Rochester Bridge's third structure, built for the old London, Chatham and Dover Railway. Rochester's river crossings are the responsibility of The Rochester Bridge Trust formed in 1398.

In the days of both sail and steam, the Medway at Strood Pier was a hive of activity. Cargo-carrying ships would anchor in this stretch of the river as well as in the Pool of Rochester further downstream.

A lone cargo vessel at a Rochester buoy provides company for a traditional Medway sailing barge.

Limehouse Reach in the 1980s. In the far distance, ships are berthed at Rochester's quaysides, but Baltic pulp ships no longer unload at midstream buoys.

Reflections of days gone by: amidst craft moored between Sun Pier and Ship Pier at Chatham is Ross Revenge *on one of her earlier visits to the Medway.*

Looking down Chatham Reach: the local paddle steamer passes Chatham's riverfront on her way to the Historic Dockyard.

Graving docks, once a vital aspect of dockyard work, are now used for the refitting of commercial vessels at Chatham.

As the flying flags show, craft of many nationalities take advantage of the Medway's safe and secure moorings.

This Thames tug looks positively tiny in its expansive dry dock within Chatham Historic Dockyard.

Seen from nearby shores, Upnor Castle keeps a watchful eye over passing shipping.

Boats, boatyards and watering holes: the picturesque riverside at Lower Upnor.

122

Like neighbouring Hoo Fort, described earlier, Darnett Fort was built in Napoleonic times to protect Chatham and its dockyard, and though recommissioned during the Second World War, it was never needed for use. It is now privately owned.

The ship jetty of Kingsnorth Power Station with a bulk carrier alongside.

Kingnorth Power Station's lofty chimney can be seen from several miles away.

Boxes upon boxes: an international array of containers stacked high on the stern of a large container ship at Thamesport.

A great way to spend a Sunday afternoon in the Medway Estuary.

Thamesport evolved on the Isle of Grain and welcomes ships operated by some of the world's major ship-owning companies. It is the Medway's only dedicated container port, so why not 'Medwayport'?

A sailing craft enhances this view of Grain Power Station, the last notable landmark on the Medway's western bank.

Ships in a line: left to right, a bulk carrier, reefer and a ro-ro forest-products carrier berthed at Sheerness.

It's farewell to the Medway as our steamer rounds Garrison Point and its passenger ferry linkspan, and enters the Thames Estuary.

Other local titles published by Tempus

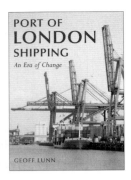

Port of London Shipping An Era of Change
GEOFF LUNN

A fascinating journey through a period of change from the latter years of London's docks up to the present day. With its wealth of illustrations, Geoff Lunn demonstrates how the Port of London has re-emerged as a premier British port, equipped to handle the most sophisticated modern ship, with further expansion planned. Millions of pounds have been spent on regeneration projects, and tourists and business people alike are using the river for leisure and commuting.

0 7524 3201 X

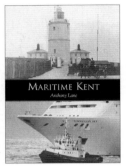

Maritime Kent
ANTHONY LANE

Maritime Kent describes the history of these different aspects of seafaring over the last two hundred years. The many photographs show how the ships have changed, and how the lives of the mariners have altered.

0 7524 1769 X

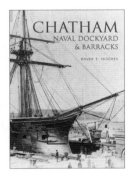

Chatham Naval Dockyard and Barracks
DAVID HUGHES

This is a fascinating volume of photographs and ephemera on the Chatham Naval Dockyard and Barracks, looking at it from its early days of existence until its role in more recent years, from the First and Second World Wars to the Falklands.

0 7524 3248 6

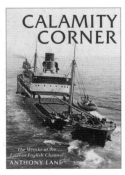

Calamity Corner: The Wrecks of the Eastern English Channel
ANTHONY LANE

For over five centuries, the English Channel's eastern approaches have seen more shipwrecks than almost any other part of the coastline. Well known for its shifting sands, narrow sea lanes and rapidly changing weather patterns, Calamity Corner illustrates just how treacherous this stretch of coast can be.

0 7524 3163 3

If you are interested in purchasing other books published by Tempus, or in case you have difficulty finding any Tempus books in your local bookshop, you can also place orders directly through our website

www.tempus-publishing.com